A
DISCIPLESHIP
PRIMER

A Guide to the Essentials of Dedication to Jesus

Trudy Pettibone

Inscript

A Division of Kingdom Christian Enterprises
PO Box 611
Bladensburg, MD 20710-0611

ISBN 978-1-957497-45-7

Inscript and the portrayal of a pen with script are trademarks of Dove Christian Publishers.

Published in the United States of America

To Linda Mellor and Joyce Jones, who took the time to review my manuscript and believed that it was worth publishing.

CONTENTS

FOREWORD

On a Monday in October of 1981, I met Jesus. It's hard to describe what happened that day. It actually started the evening before at Sunday evening church service. I felt that Jesus was trying to get my attention, so I gave it to Him. I took that Monday off work, calling in sick, which was a lie. Lying was not unusual for me at that time. It was a day of Scripture, prayer and tears, just me and Jesus. By the end of that day, I knew I was a different person. I have described my understanding of the change in me as a block of ice melting.

This converting event began in church. Church wasn't new to me. I had been in church most of my life. I had made a profession of faith some years prior and been baptized. I was even teaching Sunday School at the time of this life-changing event. I was thirty-three years old and had lived most of those years as a lie, although not an intentional one. I just knew that nothing that had ever happened at church had ever really touched my life in a deep, meaningful way. However, by the end of that Monday, I knew I would never be the same, and I haven't been.

God began working in my life immediately, and His first task was to stop my lies. I found that I had to correct myself if I said anything untrue. That was so embarrassing that it didn't take long for the lies to stop. However, over these forty-some years, the Lord has taught me that truth is about much more than not speaking lies.

I began studying scripture and praying. I started imitating people in church who had qualities that I thought honored God. God has made some of those qualities fundamental in my life. Something was missing, however. I recognized others in church who were, intentionally or unintentionally, pretending to be faithful Christians, as I had done for years. I wondered why. Most had probably made professions of faith and been baptized as I had. Their lives, like mine, were not changed.

It wasn't long before I began to discover the deficiency. People were exhorted to come forward, accept Jesus as Savior, and be baptized. They could attend Sunday School as well as worship services. We were told Christ gave us new lives, preparing us for heaven. At no point, however, neither before nor after my conversion was I aware of being taught how to receive and live out the new life that Christ gave me. What were the day-by-day practicalities of that life? Was it really just all about Sunday?

Discipleship, or the lack of such, was the answer. Jesus had people who lived and walked with Him daily, learning from Him and being prepared by Him to help others learn about Him. We call these people *disciples*. The Bible talks mostly about the twelve closest to Jesus, but there were many others.

Jesus' disciples literally followed Jesus and watched and heard his interactions with people of all identities. While they didn't really understand what Jesus was all about until his resurrection and the coming of the Holy Spirit at Pentecost, when the time came for them to lead, they were prepared because they had been with Jesus.

Today, the Church needs discipleship, which is what this book is about. We must be taught that following Jesus is a 24/7 activity involving every aspect of our lives. We need to know that learning about following Jesus starts when we accept Christ and continues into eternity. It takes work, discipline, and a commitment to being the best we can be as followers of Christ. We can be discipled by others, which I have found can be done formally and very informally. We should reach a point where we can disciple others formally in a one-on-one

Foreword

or classroom setting, or casually through friendship.

May the Lord bless you as you step out into a new understanding of your new life in Christ.

What is Discipleship?

Scriptures: Matthew 10:40-42; Luke 14:25-33

I would have liked to have taken a poll at church, a poll with one question: what do you think discipleship is? I think I would probably get as many different answers as participants. Discipleship seems to have gotten lost in church life, although it should be an integral part of life in Christ and the Church.

Discipleship is the *process* of *learning* to *follow* Jesus. That is about as simple as I can define it. Let's break down the words. First of all, it is a process. You don't become a disciple just because you accepted Christ and got baptized. Many people take those two steps but never become disciples. When we determine that we will follow Jesus, the discipling process continues until we meet Jesus in eternity. Next, we see the word "learning." Jesus spent three years teaching twelve men — and others — about what it meant to live a life that demonstrated complete love for God and others. At the time of Jesus' death, most of them did not fully get it. Only at Pentecost, when the Holy Spirit began to inhabit believers, did they truly understand what Jesus' life was about. Then, most of them spent the rest of their lives continuing to learn what it meant to follow Jesus and share that process with others.

The third keyword is "follow," which has several meanings. The first meaning is to "come after." Since we live and walk this earth in a time after Jesus, we've got that down. A second definition of "follow" is to "walk after or behind." The Twelve and others did that for three years. They heard his teachings, which we can do as we read scripture. They saw his miracles, his concern even for his enemies, and how he responded to those who ridiculed him. They watched him die with others on his mind. Unfortunately, we can't literally walk behind Jesus, but as we read the Scriptures, we can witness these acts and so many others. Faithful reading and studying of scripture are major elements of the discipleship process. Unlike the Twelve as they walked with Jesus during his life, we have the Holy Spirit who teaches as we commit to following Jesus (Acts 1:8).

The third definition of "follow" is to "do what someone else does," to copy or imitate. As we learn through scriptures all the things Jesus did and said, with the help of the indwelling Spirit, we can do and say many of those same things.

True discipleship involves changes in heart (feelings), mind (thoughts), behaviors, interests, and possibly people in our lives. It won't be easy, but honoring our Lord and Savior Jesus Christ will be very rewarding. May the Lord guide and bless you as you proceed.

We will look at two elements of discipleship related to learning to be a disciple: first, our own individual efforts toward becoming a disciple, and second, helping others learn to walk with Christ.

Learning to Walk with Christ

If you are on your own, see if the church you attend has previously had a discipleship program. If so, try to get a copy of that. Of course, if they have an ongoing discipleship program, jump right in there.

Considering all the factors of discipleship, set a program for yourself: Times, resources, goals, supplements, a progress chart, and other things particular to your life that you might want to add. Think of people you would like to talk to, books you would like to read, and maybe places you would like to visit. Look at the different arenas of your life—

home, workplace, church, family life, recreational pursuits, commerce — and think about how these will, or may not, be a part of your discipleship. Seek God's guidance in establishing your program and walking with you through each step and stage.

Helping Others to Walk with Christ

Ideally, when someone accepts Christ as Savior or gets baptized, they should immediately be put in touch with someone who has had a lengthy walk with the Lord. We will call this person a *discipler*. They should be willing and able to mentor someone and have some commonalities with the person to be discipled. There might also be a discipleship class, but each participant should have a partner in the process.

There should be a definite discipleship program, whether used in a class or with a team of two. This book will hopefully serve as a guide for discipleship, but there are other resources. On the Christianbook website, I found 13,382 results under the word "discipleship," although a quick glimpse revealed that most of these dealt with specific areas of discipleship.

Once a program is decided upon, a time frame should be set. I would advise a six-to-eight-week program. I wouldn't want to meet any less frequently than bi-weekly. This time together is to outline the basic principles of what should become a life-long process. Mentorship should continue after the established time period ends.

Questions for Consideration

1. Describe your understanding of discipleship.
2. Have you had experience in discipleship training?
3. Who are some people you know whom you would describe as disciples of Jesus?
4. Would you be willing to disciple someone else?

LIFE BEFORE CHRIST

Scriptures: Acts 8:1-3; 9:1-19; Romans 3:23

It would be easy to think that when we accept Christ into our lives, the past doesn't matter. We are forgiven for our sins and don't need to worry about what has happened before. Unfortunately, that is not true.

There are several reasons why we need to consider our past as we move forward in Christ. First of all, even though our sin is forgiven, we still often have consequences to live with. Perhaps there are children alienated from us because of our poor choices, addictions from which we must be set free, or people to whom we were unkind, from whom we need forgiveness. The Lord can give us the grace and strength to do what we must to bring healing from anything resulting from actions before we met Christ.

Secondly, while we can't live in the past and be haunted by its shadows, looking at our past in light of what God has done for us in Christ can often be valuable. I can reflect on the attitudes I used to have and rejoice that those attitudes are no longer part of my life. Also, as I look back on my past, I can see how God worked in my life, especially protecting me from things that could have destroyed my life. God knew and loved me and worked in my life long before I met Christ.

Finally, we can look at our past to see what God might be able to use in our present and our future. Following is a list of some things we might consider.

Interests and Hobbies

In the 3rd grade, I had a teacher, Miss Seekamp, who encouraged me to write little essays to read at "Show and Tell" time because I was very shy. That began my interest in writing, which the Lord has used in various ways.

I grew up in a household with an artistic father and brothers. Although I had no talent in that area, I always sought an artistic outlet for my jealousy and frustration. As an adult, I discovered that I could copy a model and create a greeting card that the Lord could use to touch a life. I knew I had found a niche.

Examine your interests and hobbies and see if there is something that God can use to touch other lives for Christ and maybe even to enhance your own walk with the Lord.

Strengths and Weaknesses

Do you know your personal strengths and weaknesses? If not, ask the Lord to reveal them to you. You may not like what you are shown, but don't let that discourage you.

It is easy to see how God can use our strengths. Almost any positive ability or trait can be surrendered to God for God's use. Are you an athlete (I've got basketball on TV right now), a good speaker, a gifted fundraiser, a writer, or a strong financial manager? Do you make friends or peace easily? Do you play a musical instrument? Are exercise, meditation, or reading important to you? God can use all these abilities and strengths and many more for the Kingdom if surrendered for God's purposes.

Seeing how God might use our weaknesses is a little more difficult. I can give one example from my life. I see social conversation as my greatest weakness. If you put me in a social setting, I won't talk much. What I am going to do is listen. Good listeners are invaluable for God's Kingdom. When we listen to people, we know how to pray for them. We hear ways in which we can minister to people. If I talked all the time, I would miss out on many opportunities for prayer. Examine your weaknesses and see how the result of those weaknesses might be used for God's Kingdom.

High Points

What are the high points of your life before Christ? A wedding, the birth of a child, a major career accomplishment, or a community award might be on your list. Look back at these events. How did they happen? What were some surprises? How did you feel? Who shared these times with you? How did you work through any difficult times that may have been involved in these high points? Pray as you consider these things, asking God to show you how He was involved in each one. We need to remember that even though we might not be thinking about God, He was right there, walking with us through the special moments of our lives.

Low Points

The lowest point of my life before I met Jesus was the death of my father. I've never loved anyone as much as I loved my father. I was nineteen, unmarried, and pregnant. My mother had kicked me out of the house, and I was living out of town, so I didn't know how sick my father was. A police officer came to where I was and told me I needed to go home. I went home that day and found Dad in bed. We talked for a while, and I left. Later that night, Dad was rushed to the hospital. I never saw him alive again. I can look back on that time and see how God brought me through the shock, devastating grief, and some anger at my mother. God eventually helped me forgive my mother. No matter what we face apart from Christ, we are not alone. Although I felt very much alone, I know now that God was with me at that difficult time, comforting, strengthening, and guiding me, maybe even preparing me to face future grief, such as the suicide of two grandsons.

Regrets and Fond Remembrances

When we enter our new life in Christ, it is important that we not dwell on our past. We have seen how a limited review of the past can serve a purpose in helping us discover our potential for our present and future in Christ. However, to try to live in the past conflicts with the love and mercy of God, which are new every morning (Lamentations 3:22-23).

So, how do we deal with our regrets about things we did in the past, regrets that the enemy might use to try and defeat us in our new walk with the Lord? First of all, we have to recognize that effort. The enemy would like nothing more than to keep us embedded in past sorrows and regrets so that we might miss what God wants to do in us today.

Secondly, we should seek forgiveness for the cause of our regrets. First of all, accept God's forgiveness of all that you have confessed to God (and don't forget continued confession of sin that may enter your life. 1 John 1:9). Then, if possible, seek forgiveness from others for the harm you may have done to them. Finally, don't forget to forgive yourself. That may be the most difficult forgiveness of all, but it can bring the greatest reward.

Thirdly, when regrets come to mind, ask God to help you put them aside and remind the enemy that you don't have to pay attention to things God has forgiven.

It is very easy to think that it is okay to dwell on good memories (fond remembrances). Very often, it might be a good thing to remember a special time. That can be comforting in difficult times. Again, however, God worked in our lives yesterday and wants to continue His work today and tomorrow. If we are focused on "then," even on good things, we will miss what God wants to do *now*. The past is gone. Open the door for what God wants to do in the present and future. When you find yourself dwelling on fond remembrances, God can help you come back to the present, which may offer an even fonder remembrance.

Your Need for Christ

As I said before, I had been in church most of my life before I met Christ. I don't know what I would have said had I been asked about my Christian life. In my preteen years, I sang, and I helped the pastor and his wife with various things. I probably would have thought I was a pretty good Christian.

As I entered my teen years, I began to notice what I considered hypocrisy at church. One example is the youth leaders who couldn't wait to get out the door to light up their cigarettes. I dropped out for a while. Unfortunately, so did my life. In my early twenties, I began seeking. I attended a church where I first heard of accepting Christ as my Savior. Since I couldn't be part of anything in that church unless I joined, I made a profession of faith and was baptized. For the next 10 to 15 years, I attended various churches on and off. I didn't like my life, and I didn't like myself. I got divorced and sent three of my four children to live with their father.

I don't know how I got to the church I was part of when I first met Christ. Somewhere in that 10–13-year period, I realized that church attendance wasn't doing anything for me. Having church members as friends wasn't doing anything for me. Even teaching Sunday School wasn't doing anything for me, and I shouldn't have been doing that anyway at that time in my life. I knew I needed something more. When I got to that point, Christ came to me.

As a layperson and a minister, I have recognized many people who walked a similar path to mine. Many never realized what they truly needed. It wasn't church attendance, singing in the choir, writing nice checks for the offering plate, wearing your best clothes, playing on the church baseball team, or even being part of a church ministry team. What every single person who has ever walked this earth needs is Jesus.

It's not enough to read about Jesus or hear him preached about. It's not enough to sing about Jesus or teach about Jesus. It's not enough to be in church every Sunday of your life or even every Sunday and Wednesday evening. It's not even enough to be a "good" person, however that may be defined.

We need to enter into and live our lives in relationship with Jesus. Jesus needs to be more real to us than the closest flesh-and-blood people in our lives. We need to do the same things with Jesus that we do with touchable people that we love: learn all we can about Him, think about Him constantly, spend time with Him, and talk to and about Him. We need to give Jesus our best time, effort, and resources. We need to remember that Jesus is always with us and knows our most hidden deeds and thoughts. As we grow in our relationship with Jesus, hidden deeds and thoughts should disappear. Language and speech, along with attitudes and behaviors, should change. Our love for Jesus and all others should increase noticeably. Pleasing Jesus should become the overriding priority of our lives, and we have the power of the Holy Spirit to make that happen. We need Jesus Christ every microsecond of our existence, and we are blessed with the ability to make that happen.

Questions for Consideration

1. What things in your past might be detrimental to following Christ?

2. What from your past might be useful as you follow Christ?
3. Do you know your personal strengths and weaknesses?
4. Can you forgive yourself for things you have done that do not honor Christ?

YOUR NEW LIFE

*Scriptures: Matthew 4:18-22; John 3:1-20; Romans 6:23; 2
Corinthians 5:17; Philippians 3:7-11; 1 John 5:10-12*

Many people have disagreed with me, but I believe that our new life in Christ must have a definite beginning, a time that we can look to and know without a shadow of a doubt that we received Christ as our Savior. Just as there are indications that this has happened, there are also indications that it has not. We will look at examples of both.

Receiving Christ as Savior doesn't happen just because we have Christian parents, have been baptized/christened, or go to church all the time. There are certain criteria. One, we must be old enough to understand what Christ did for us on the cross and how that personally impacts us. Two, once we hear the gospel and understand its significance, we must make a definite, informed decision to receive Christ as our Savior. And three, we must sincerely ask Christ to be our Savior, acknowledging our sins and receiving forgiveness.

These criteria can be met in different ways. As we see with Saul in Acts 9, Christ coming into our lives can be a very dramatic event. That's not how it is for most people. However, there should be some clear signs that our new life has begun. As Jesus told Nicodemus in John 3, we must be born again. That is the start. Let's look at what could or should follow.

When It Began

As I said before, I can trace the beginning of my conversion to a Monday in October of 1981. I knew at the end of that day that I was a different person. It wasn't long before God began changing some specific things in my life, but my awareness of the Holy Spirit was almost instant.

Can you look back to a time when, intentionally and with understanding, you welcomed Christ into your life? What changes started happening around that time? Where were you? Were people in your life commenting on things in your life that they saw as different? If you can't identify such a definite time in your life, maybe you haven't received Christ. 2 Corinthians 5:17 says that if we are in Christ, old things pass away, and all things become new. We become a new creation. That scripture indicates a distinct change that we must experience.

How It Happened

There are many ways in which conversion can begin. Some are very dramatic and public such as that which happened to Saul, who became Paul (Acts 9). I was at home, alone with Jesus. No bright lights, no trumpet blast. With a heart heavy with the sense of my sin, I, as sincere as I have ever been, asked Jesus to save me. I had done that before with no results. This time was very different.

Many people receive Christ in a church setting, either during worship or maybe in a Sunday School/Bible study class. For others, it happens in a counseling session with a pastor or another minister. We might be alone or surrounded by people, but there must be some event that precipitates our conversion.

If you can't remember a time or event that resulted in a change in your life, I'd like to suggest an activity. Find the time and space to get alone with the Lord with a notebook and a pen. Ask the Lord to take you on a journey back through your life or at least to the time when you started to go to church. Identify special times or activities; for example, why did you start going to church? This may seem silly, but if you are sincerely seeking, the Lord will help you find the starting point. Just like the fishermen that Jesus told to follow him, which was the start of their discipleship, we need a starting point in our discipleship. Jesus calls, and we have to decide to follow. When and how did that happen for you?

Instant Changes

The first definite change in my life was when the Lord made me stop telling lies, and that was within a week of that incredible Monday. Over the years, I have learned that being a person of truth goes way beyond not speaking lies. Hypocrisy, innuendo, hidden motives, insincerity, and so many more things will be present in a life not devoted to truth. The Lord has worked with me to rid my life of such things, but He started with one thing almost instantly.

When someone truly receives Christ, I think they will begin to recognize some change very quickly. Maybe it's a change in friendship, a way of thinking, or a habit that they lose interest in pursuing. Look for little things that will begin a lifelong transformation.

Rejection and Acceptance

As we begin our walk with the Lord and our transformation progresses, we will see different responses from people in our lives. Early on in my walk, when I was only aware of the lying that was no longer in my life, people started commenting on the changes they saw in me. If they didn't say something specific, I didn't ask. These were mostly people at church.

There was one member of my family who did not accept what Christ was doing in my life and what I was sharing about that. They felt it was all unnecessary, that a moral or ethical life was all that was needed to get to heaven.

My witnessing about the Lord in my life got me in trouble. I was a paralegal for a law firm. I talked about Jesus during breaks and other free time. I got fired, the one and only time in my life. My work was good behind the scenes, but when they sent me to do closings, I didn't converse as they wanted me to. I am sure being fired was also partly because of my witness. I know I made people uncomfortable.

Unless people are really set against the Lord, the new life the Lord is creating in us should be accepted by most. We do have to be careful about how we witness for Jesus, and I will address that in Chapter 8.

Your Support Team

One of the things I think is so important, especially in our early walk with the Lord, is to have a strong, Godly support team. It can consist of friends or family who may or may not go to your church. I formed a group of friends in the church I was attending when I met Christ, and I think they were very supportive. As I grew in the Lord, however, I came to notice things in the church that I saw as a signal that I needed to find another church. I never really found another support team.

People who will pray with and for us, celebrate our joys, join us in our sorrows, and listen to us and share their stories are invaluable. Every disciple of Jesus should find such a group.

Discouragement

One of the saddest things I have seen in church life involves new followers of Christ. They are on fire for the Lord, talking to everyone who will listen about Jesus. However, sometimes they encounter a friend or family member who does everything to discourage the new disciple. They may withhold elements of their relationship or be constantly critical of the new believer. They may even end the relationship. This response so discourages the new believer that they begin to lose their faith. They may even stop going to church and start denying Jesus.

Of course, the believer may respond by questioning whether they truly accepted Jesus, but it's not that simple. Scripture tells us of disciples who turned away and stopped following Jesus (e.g., John 6:66). When we are not firmly grounded in our faith, it is not surprising that we might turn away. God, however, can defeat the discouragement that the enemy wants to bring into our lives. God can also turn back those who turn away. Philippians 2:12 tells us to work out our own salvation with fear and trembling. Unfortunately, that may be fear of how the people we love respond.

Encouragement

Nothing can lift the spirits of a new believer more than someone commenting that they like the changes they see in them. This isn't likely if we hide our lamps under a bushel. The more we live out what the Lord has put in us, the more we bear witness to the work Christ is doing in our lives, the more likely we are to hear words of encouragement.

I wasn't really aware of it, but I must have been a pretty critical person before Christ came into my life. That has changed, but it has only happened in recent years. Actually, only in the past two or so years have I realized that I have become an encourager. Not only do negative words not come from my lips, but even negative thoughts are rare. It doesn't stop there. I find myself speaking positive words of encouragement even to strangers. The biggest surprise is how I speak with my family. I am sure, or I certainly hope, that they have been surprised by my observations and responses.

I am just beginning to realize how a positive attitude, accompanied by words of encouragement, can be effective not only to encourage new believers, but even to win people to Christ. Romans 15:5 calls God a "God of endurance and encouragement." If we have a God who is encouraging us in our new lives, we, with the help of God's Spirit within, can learn to bring encouragement to others.

All Things New

The new life that we are given when we receive Christ as Savior can and should be all-encompassing. We are going to focus on newness in chapter seven, but there are a few things to touch on now.

As we consider ourselves a new creation, we might think along the lines of a new plant. In a recent televised sermon, the Rev. Dr. Tony Evans said that the seed of God's nature is implanted in us at conversion. Just as a plant seed contains the full potential of the plant, so we who have received Christ have all the fullness of God within us. When a seed is planted, water, fertilizer, sunshine, and freedom from weeds help that seed grow into a strong, healthy plant.

How do we help the new nature grow within us? First of all, it should be a daily discipline of care, and we will look at that in chapter four. The study of scripture and prayer are the water and fertilizer. Regular worship and fellowship with other believers can provide the light that represents the sunshine. And we weed by pulling out of our lives the thoughts, attitudes, speech, and habits that do not honor God.

It is important to remember that, according to Ephesians 2:8-9, we are saved by grace through faith, not works, lest anyone boast. When we think about things like watering, fertilizing, and weeding, it seems like work, and it is. Developing new disciplines is not easy. Philippians 2:12-13 tells us to "work out our own salvation," but two things are important to remember here. One, it says "work out," not "work for." We are to take what God has put in and bring it to reality in our lives. Secondly, we don't have to do this alone. This Scripture says it is God who is working in us to will and work for God's great pleasure.

Questions for Consideration

1. Can you identify definite evidence in your life that you have been born again?
2. Have people commented on changes they see in your life since you were born again?
3. Have you felt free to share what God has done in your life?
4. Do you have people with whom you can share, pray for, and be prayed for?
5. What do you do to nourish your new life in Christ?

DEDICATE THE TIME

Scriptures: Acts 2:42-47; Ephesians 3:14-21

Now, we are getting to the nuts and bolts of daily life as a disciple of Jesus Christ. The first is the setting aside of a special time each day to meet with the Lord. This time serves several purposes: First, a special time indicates that Jesus is a priority in our lives. Second, as with the flesh-and-blood people of our lives, time together strengthens our relationship. Next, we aren't very likely to grow in faith and practice without taking time to study the manual of faith and practice, the Bible. Finally, time spent with the Lord sets the tone for the day.

As a new pastor, I was appalled to learn that some of my peers did not think it was necessary to spend time with the Lord other than their sermon preparation. As I got to know these people, I could see the evidence of a lack of relationship-building with Jesus. I can't stress enough the need for this set-apart time.

Time spent with God is often called quiet time, but it need not always be quiet. I pray out loud, and sometimes I sing. I also like to read out loud some scriptures, especially the Psalms. That may be because so many of the Psalms seem like or are indeed prayers. I also do a lot of reading and writing.

A Set Time Each Day

I once tried praying and reading the Bible in the evening. It didn't work for me. I was distracted by the day's memories, and I wasn't focusing on Jesus.

I've always been more of a morning person, so having a morning quiet time worked for me, even though I had to get up earlier than I liked. You wake up with a clear mind. The day lies ahead, and you can make a difference in that day by starting it with the Lord.

There are 49 references in scripture to people rising early in the morning to be about God's work. While God may be available to us 24/7, we are not as available to God. There may, of course, be times within which we can't meet with God at a regular time, but that should always be our goal.

A Commitment to Relationship

A quiet time each day can serve many purposes. Maybe we want to memorize some Scripture or prepare for Sunday School class. Maybe we heard something we want to check on in the Scriptures. Or maybe we feel that a few minutes a day in Bible reading or prayer is something we are supposed to do.

While all those things might be good, they are not the main reasons for daily quiet time. From Exodus through Numbers, we see mention of a Tent of Meeting. This was the place that was established for worship, but it was also the place where Moses met and continued his relationship with God at special times. A special time set apart for the Lord is intended to build our relationship with the Lord. Remember the basic elements of a relationship?

(1) *We want to get to know someone.* We can learn more about Jesus by reading and studying scripture. Devotional books by respected leaders in the faith can also help.

(2) *We talk to someone we are in relationship with.* We do this during a formal prayer time, but we can also talk to Jesus throughout the day. (3) *We think about people we are in relationship with.* We can meditate on the scriptures and other

readings throughout the day.

(4) *We listen to people we are in relationship with.* Jesus will speak to us if we give him the opportunity. He speaks through Scripture but will also speak directly to our hearts. We only have to take the time to listen.

(5) *We spend time with people we are in relationship with.* God is present everywhere, but are we always present with God? Whether we are at church, home, or anywhere else, we can be in the proximity of God without being present to God.

Finally, (6) *We want to let others know about the ones with whom we are in relationship.* When we spend dedicated time with the Lord daily, we are much better prepared to tell others about all He has done for us.

I believe that a faithful, ongoing relationship with the Lord is a great foundation for our flesh-and-blood relationships. As we learn about and get to know Jesus, we learn how to treat others. Jesu gave us two commandments: First, love God with all our being—heart, soul, mind, and strength. The second is to love our neighbor as ourselves (Mark 12:30-31). I believe that how well we are doing the second indicates whether we are doing the first.

A Special Place

Just as Moses met with God in a special place, the Tent of Meeting, we should have a special place to meet with God. I used to be very particular about where I sat during my quiet time. For years, the notebooks filled with notes on my devotional readings and prayers were called "From the Chair." Then I moved and haven't really had a special place.

Some criteria for a special place for your quiet time might be:

(1) a place that is quiet, where there won't be a lot of distracting noise;

(2) an out-of-the-way place where the family can go about their business without mutual distractions. This is especially important if you pray or read out loud. I want my family to know I was praying, but not necessarily to know what I was praying about, and

(3) a comfortable place. At one point, I had a hammock-like swing in the basement. Be careful not to be too comfortable.

Also, it would be convenient to have a place nearby where you can find your devotional tools.

Tools of Devotion

There are certain things you really should have on hand as you begin your quiet time. The first thing, of course, should be a good Bible translation. Paraphrases, like *The Message*, can be helpful for clarification. I like actual translations, such as NIV or NASB. Each of these comes in an updated version. King James (KJV) is great for memorization but maybe not the best for reading or study. More in chapter five.

It is not very much a part of my quiet time today, but for years, I have kept a notebook nearby to record questions and comments as I read Scripture. A handy-dandy notebook can be very helpful. Along with notes from reading, you might also want to keep track of what you are praying about.

There are countless devotional books available. One I have used for decades is Oswald Chambers' *My Utmost for His Highest*. Currently, I use it every other year and fill in with various other devotionals. I often use more than one devotional at a time. Currently, I have one devotional, which is accompanied by a workbook. I am using both of these plus *Utmost*. I can think of no better book for discipleship than Chambers' book. It would be impossible for me to describe the changes the Lord has worked in my life through the writings of Oswald Chambers.

Dedicate the Time

Years ago, the Lord put a prayer ministry on my heart. I started making a list of people to pray for. My family, the church I was part of, and our nation have long been the subjects of my daily prayers. I started noting the names of people we met as we traveled the country. Wherever I was, there seemed to be people the Lord led me to put on my list. I would often pray in their presence and then add them to the list. Now, my prayer list is divided into more than ten sections, with forty to fifty names in each section. Each day, following my daily prayers, I pray for the names in one section of my list. Whether or not you feel led to a prayer ministry, I would definitely advise a prayer list or journal. When we don't have the means to reach out and touch lives directly, prayer is the best thing we can do for anyone at any time.

Finally, I would like to recommend keeping a prayer journal. A book that allows for several years of entries is most desirable. As I make today's entry of petitions, thanksgiving, and praise, I can look back to what I was praying for in years past. Currently, my journal goes back to 2020. It is wonderful to reflect on how the Lord answered those prayers.

Questions for Consideration

1. Do you dedicate a special time each day to the Lord?
2. How are you building your relationship with the Lord?
3. Do you have confidence in the tools you might use to build your relationship with the Lord?

MAKE SCRIPTURE YOURS

Scriptures: Psalm 119:1-8, 11, 105 (actually, all of Psalm 119 is about scripture); Hebrews 4:12; 2 Timothy 3:16

Apart from beginning our relationship with Jesus by trusting Him as our Savior, nothing is more important to discipleship than Scripture. Through Scripture, we learn about God's work with humanity from creation in Genesis through the re-creation of a new heaven and earth described in Revelation. We see stories of God's protection, guidance, discipline, provision, and vengeance, all enveloped in God's love. The "highlight" event, the Passion of Christ, involving His arrest, trial, crucifixion, and resurrection, shows God's mercy and grace extended to all humanity. The development and growth of the Church, the Body of Christ (1 Corinthians 12:27), as described in the Book of Acts, and the letters written for the edification of members give us clear guidance on how we should live.

Reading Scripture

I have heard about "Read the Bible in a Year" reading plans but have not participated in them. If you plan to take each day's section and meditate on it, form questions about it, and research words or ideas that are new to you or that you don't understand, then such reading can be beneficial. That, however, does not match my understanding of how people usually use such programs.

If you are reading the Bible because you think you are

supposed to or to say that you are reading it, then you probably are not getting a lot out of it. The Bible is our manual for Godliness. We need to have a system of reading Scripture that will give us an understanding of God's work for us, within us, and through us.

Start with one book. The Gospel of John is, I believe, a great beginning, especially with discipleship in mind. Don't read it by chapter; read it by paragraphs if your Bible is divided by such. Note—and I would suggest, journal—the following:

1. Who is speaking? Narrator, Deity, Character.
2. Who is being spoken to?
3. What is the main idea of the paragraph?
4. How does this apply to you?
5. What is the response of the hearers?

When you feel you understand the paragraph well, move on to the next, making the appropriate connections. Continue this process through the chapter. Then, go back and summarize the chapter, noting the following:

1. Main ideas,
2. Connections and breaks;
3. Common themes;
4. Differing themes;
5. People involved: Actions, Comments, Responses
6. Significance to you.

Some tools helpful for these studies might be a Bible handbook, commentaries, dictionary/concordance (Bible), and a Bible thesaurus.

Memorizing Scripture

Reading, meditating on, and studying Scripture are very important for practical understanding and are required for faithful discipleship. Memorizing particular scriptures can supplement the general understanding of all of Scripture. There are several ways of doing this.

There are several Scripture memorization programs or agendas. One I remember is the *Roman Road*. This program focuses on various Scriptures related to our salvation, such as Romans 3:23 and 6:23. You might add to these John 3:16, Ephesians 2:8-9, and 2 Corinthians 5:17, among others.

I think a personalized program is best. It is based on the interests and needs of the individual doing the memorizing. A Bible concordance can help you find particular scriptures based on a theme or word. After making a list of relevant verses, work on one at a time.

The King James Version can be very helpful for memorization. The different words and syntax make memorizing easy for most people. After memorizing from King James, learn the Scriptures from your favorite translation. Paraphrases may not be great for memorizing. Psalm 119:11 talks about storing up or hiding God's word in our hearts. Memorizing helps us do this.

Group Study

I can't think of a more effective way of studying and learning the Scriptures than with a group. I'm not talking about a topical study or gender-based study that may or may not focus on Scripture. I'm not even talking about a video study, at least not most that I have seen.

The most effective way to study Scripture is one Biblical book at a time. It should be expository, verse by verse, if possible. Some books of the Bible, like Psalms and Revelation, might lend themselves to a topical study, but the Scripture, not the theme or the experiences of members of the group, must be the main focus.

Some very well-prepared Bible studies can reduce the preparation work for the leader. Three that I recommend are *NavPress*, *John MacArthur*, and *Smyth and Helwys*.

The benefits of studying with a group are numerous. A few benefits I have experienced are varying understandings and opinions, the creation of a fellowship, and mutual affirmation. There will always be someone who does more work than others, and what these people bring to the group can be invaluable.

Worship Services

Many people have attended church on Sunday for most of their lives and still do not know the Bible. They might be familiar with a few verses but do not know Scripture as a whole. Early in my faith walk, I started taking the Scripture from Sunday morning worship and studying it on my own at home. This gave me a very good foundation.

There are pastors who are good Bible teachers and pastors who are not. I prefer expository preaching. These pastors will take a reasonable length of passage and essentially preach verse by verse. Some do a mediocre job. However, if you find a truly inspired pastor who knows and loves Scripture, Sunday worship can become a very meaningful source of Bible study, especially if you take notes and follow up with your own study at home.

Questions for Consideration

1. Do you follow a particular bible reading program?
2. Have you memorized any scripture?
3. Do you have Bible study tools such as a Bible handbook, concordance, or thesaurus?
4. Have you considered or are you part of a Bible study group?

WHY CHURCH?

Scriptures: Psalm 78:1-4; 1 Corinthians 1:4-9; 2 Corinthians 6:14-18

Where We Can and Should Meet Jesus

As I said previously, I've been in church most of my life. For the first 33 years of my life, it had little effect. But while I was attending a Sunday night service—probably because most of my friends were there—Jesus began to speak to me. Would that have happened if I hadn't been in church? Only God knows, but it is very important to me that it *did* happen in church, or at least that is where our encounter started. It continued through the night and into the next day. By the end of that Monday, I knew I was a different person.

The most important thing that can happen in church is that we meet Jesus. Of course, there are a lot of other things that can happen at church: we can make friends, maybe meet our soul mate, we can find our importance in the ways in which we serve, and we can find pride in the fact that we go to church. However, if we don't meet Jesus, none of that really matters. Knowing Jesus is the most important thing that can ever happen to any person. If you doubt that, chances are good that you haven't really met Jesus.

It's true that we can meet Jesus outside of church. We can meet Jesus anywhere, and the encounter can be just as real and significant as if it had happened at church. Whenever and wherever we have that initial encounter, it should lead us to church.

Many people think they can be Christians and worship apart from church attendance. I've tried that, but it's just not true! 1 Corinthians 12:27 says that we are the Body of Christ and, individually, members of that Body. Ephesians 5:23 says specifically that Christ is the head of the Church, His Body. Body parts cannot sever themselves from the Body and expect to function properly.

The Church is more than a social or civic organization. It is not a club. Church is the gathering together of believers in Jesus Christ. Yes, there are people who attend the gathering who do not know Jesus, but the goal should always be that they meet and commit to living for the One who gave His life for them.

Studying Opportunities

Through church attendance, we are given opportunities to learn about Jesus and how to follow Him. It amazes me that so few people take advantage of these opportunities.

Sunday mornings in many churches, there are classes called Sunday School, or, for the "more mature," they may be called Bible Study. I like Sunday School, maybe because I love being a student. Ideally, the Bible is studied thoroughly, one book at a time. I know of a class that has been in the book of Matthew for months. In these classes, there should always be discussion, which, I believe, is a great opportunity for learning.

Then, throughout the week, there should be varying opportunities to study scriptures. All scripture is profitable for teaching and training in righteousness (2 Timothy 3:16), but for discipleship, I feel that scriptures such as the Gospels and the epistles are the most effective since they reveal Jesus to us in many ways.

There are gatherings that are called Bible Studies but are not really Bible studies. Often, they are life studies that happen to include the Bible. Sometimes, there are studies of concepts or theories. If the concept relates to Jesus and is grounded in scripture, that could be a very significant study.

A person truly interested in being a disciple of Jesus will participate in church-related studies about Jesus and how to follow Him. Such a person should also be able to evaluate the value of such studies.

Fellowship with Other Believers

Christine Caine, author of *Don't Look Back,* quotes Jennie Allen in saying that "God existed in relationship with himself before any of us were here. It's called the Trinity."[1] God exists in relationship with Godself and invites us into that relationship through Christ. Relationship is very important to God and should be important to us.

We can find and make friends anywhere. I acknowledge that making friends as an adult—especially a single adult—is not easy for me. I have been in my current—and, hopefully, last—church for almost a year now and am really just starting to form friendships. The beautiful thing about this is that these friendships are eternal. We can't really say that about friendships outside of the Body of Christ.

Worldly friendships can offer us much: companionship, social advantages, and career advancement, to name a few. Friendships formed within the Body of Christ can offer many of the same things. The one thing a faith-based friendship can offer that a worldly friendship can't offer is the mutuality of hearts, minds, and bodies committed to Christ. To have a friend who shares one's walk with Christ is invaluable. That doesn't mean we will always think, talk, or act alike, but in

---

1 Jennie Allen "Find Your People. Building Deep Community in a Lonely World" 1st ed. (Colorado Springs: WaterBrook, 2022), 23.

Christ, we have a mediator who can help us reconcile our differences.

Witnessing Christ in Action

Many of us have seen Christ, but we may not have recognized Him. He was in a warm smile, a kind word, a welcoming attitude, a small financial assist to someone in need, or a hand offered to lift someone up. Christ can be seen in food pantry distributions, church-wide work days in the community, or teamwork on a softball field.

Through churches, we see Christ in action. A church that is not revealing Christ to its community and members is barely worthy of the name. Jesus commanded His followers to go forth and make disciples (Matthew 28:19). If Christ is only being preached from the pulpit and not being taken home and brought forth into the world, not only are we not making disciples, but we also aren't being very good disciples either.

Questions for Consideration

1. How important to you is church attendance?
2. How would you define Church?
3. What are your favorite aspects of church life?
4. How have you seen Christ in church life?

LIVING THE DIFFERENCES

Scriptures: Psalm 19:14; Romans 13:8-14; Galatians 5:16-26;
Ephesians 6:10-20

When we come to Christ, we become new creatures (2 Corinthians 5:17), which means new ways of thinking, talking, and acting. It could mean new friends, new activities, maybe new employment. Some of these changes might be instant, and some may happen over a period of years, but if we have truly been born again, changes will take place.

What Has to Change

Oswald Chambers says that "no one is ever united with Jesus Christ until he is willing to relinquish not sin only, but his whole way of looking at things."[2] The important thing to remember about change is that we do not have to do it alone. We have the power of the indwelling Holy Spirit to reveal what needs to change, guide us into that change, and help us accomplish the change. Our part is to submit to the leadership of the Lord through the Spirit.

Each morning, as I put on the Armor of God (Ephesians 6:10-20), I have certain prayers I include with each part. For instance, when I take the breastplate of righteousness, I ask the Lord to help me walk worthy of the righteousness imputed to me (2 Corinthians 5:21). To me, this means living for that day in a way that honors God. I think this is a good way to

2 "My Utmost for His Highest; Welsh Publishing, NIV Edition, copyright 1935 by Dodd, Mead & Company 1935, Pg. 49

approach a transformed life.

Start by making a list of things in your life that do not honor God. Consider the activities you engage in, the friends you hang out with, the thoughts that you let linger in your mind, the language you use, the things you watch and listen to, and the way you approach your daily activities. As you identify things that you believe need to be changed, commit these to prayer. Of course, it is very likely that the Holy Spirit has already convicted you of certain things. If you can't think of anything in your life that needs to change, then I suggest that you spend more time in prayer. No one, saved or otherwise, is so right in God's sight that there is nothing that needs changing. On the other hand, if you feel that everything needs to change, then more prayer might also be in order, as well as a Spirit-guided list of the positive things in your life.

The first thing the Lord changed in my life after I met Jesus was my habit of lying. That change was almost instant. Over the intervening years, the Lord has taught me that truth is about much more than not intentionally speaking lies. Now, when I witness or discern untruth in any form, whether with people in movies and TV or in real life, I become very agitated. That is what transformation looks like—a completely different way of perceiving, receiving, and responding.

What Might be Preferable to Change

There might be things in your life that don't actually dishonor God but that you may feel need to be changed. This could apply to any number of things. They aren't really sinful, but you just don't feel comfortable with them in your life, considering your new relationship with Jesus. Be very careful about making such changes without prayer. Since God can transform the sinful things in our lives, God can certainly use those things which are not sinful.

Living the Differences

Two areas of transformation that need special attention are our friendships and the things in our lives that may not be readily visible. We will address these in the rest of this chapter.

Old Friends, New Friends

One of the most difficult aspects of discipleship is that we may have to abandon long-time friendships. That doesn't mean we stop loving someone. Love is our primary mandate as we follow Jesus. What a new life in Christ might mean is that we can't maintain friendships that were important to us because of the foundation of those friendships.

In her book "Don't Look Back," Christine Caine provides a list of qualities we should look for in our friends if we want to be faithful to Christ. She says we should ask the Lord to help us find friends who:

1. Stick closer than a brother (Proverbs 18:24);
2. Love at all times (Proverbs 17:17);
3. Have Godly character (1 Corinthians 15:33);
4. Forgive easily (Colossians 3:13);
5. Are tenderhearted (Ephesians 4:32);
6. Won't judge (James 4:11);
7. Will help you carry what's heavy (Galatians 6:2);
8. Will confront and sort through misunderstandings (Col. 3:12-14);
9. Are reliable (Proverbs 25:13,MSG; Luke 11:5-8);
10. Will keep your confidence (Proverbs 16:28, 17:9);
11. Are wise (Proverbs 13:20); and,
12. Will encourage you and build you up (1 Thessalonians 5:11).[3]

---

3 Christine Caine, Don't Look Back, Nelson Books Publishing, Copyright 2023 by Caso Writing LIC, pg. 54.

It would seem to be a good idea to weigh all friendships by Caine's scale. The overriding quality, of course, would be a relationship with Jesus Christ.

Not Just Actions

As we so often see in the Scriptures, the people who were believed by people to be closest to God were often very far from God. Jesus describes this phenomenon in Matthew 23:25-33. Jesus described the Scribes and Pharisees as hypocrites, blind, and similar to white-washed tombs. They legalistically performed all the outer criteria for Godliness but were not obedient to God inwardly. Being a disciple of Christ is an inward position as well as an outward position.

Oswald Chambers talks about separation. In the Old Testament, Abraham and his immediate family were physically separated from family and loved ones as they sought to follow God. Beginning in Genesis, chapter 11, we see the story of Abram, whose name God changed to Abraham. In chapter 12, God calls him to leave his kindred and his father's house to the land God would show him. That was a physical separation. Chambers says, "Today, the separation is more of a mental and moral separation from the way that those who are dearest to us look at things, that is if they have not a personal relationship with God."[4] Jesus reinforces this idea in Luke 14:26. Our love for the Lord should, by comparison, seem like hatred, even for our closest family members.

Being a disciple of Jesus is not just about what we do. It is about how we think, feel, and secretly respond to things. What movies and TV do we watch? What do we allow into our minds through the eye gates and ear gates?

Physical and exterior actions are important. In the book of James, chapter 2, we read that faith without works is dead

4 Chambers, pg. 56

(verse 17). If we are true disciples of Jesus, it will be evident by our behavior and by our exterior life. What people see on the outside, however, cannot be all there is.

I have tried to walk faithfully with the Lord for 40 years. Many of my exterior behaviors have changed with the Lord's help and guidance. However, I still struggle with some of my thoughts, attitudes, and responses. The Lord is teaching me about love, something I realized was absent from my life for years. Learning to love has been critical not only in how I treat people but also in how I think and talk about people. Jesus gave two commandments: to love God with all our being—heart, soul, mind, and strength; and to love our neighbors as ourselves (Mark 12:29-31). I truly believe that how well we do the second is an indication of whether we are truly doing the first. Love will be shown by actions but also by our thoughts and attitudes.

Questions for Consideration

1. What are some new things in your life that are the result of your transformation in Christ?
2. Have you identified what might need to change in your life?
3. Are there friendships that have changed or might need to change because of your new life in Christ?

What Do You Know?

Scriptures: Romans 5, 6 and 8

Discipleship is following Jesus and helping others learn about and follow Jesus. So, how do we know what to believe and what to do? How do we know what to share with others? There are three sources: the Scriptures, our experiences, and what we have seen God do in the lives of others. Scriptures are, by far, the greatest authority, but some experiences cannot be neglected as far as demonstrating God's work in the lives of people, both believers and others.

What do the Scriptures Say?

We all know that John 3:16 tells us about God's great love for the world (God's creation), love so great that it sent God's beloved son to the cross so that believers might have eternal life. This verse has been called the Gospel in a nutshell. Why did Jesus have to go to the cross? How did that affect us? What does it mean to believe? What if we don't believe? All of these questions and many more can be answered through the Scriptures.

It would be nice to be able to list all the scriptures that might answer our questions about believing in and living for Jesus, but that would be cumbersome. The three chapters in Romans that I have placed at the beginning of this chapter are a good starting place. Additionally, I am going to list some scriptures that I feel are essential for walking with the Lord and understanding that walk so we can help others understand.

A Discipleship Primer

1. <u>Romans 3:23.</u> Not a single person who has ever walked this earth, except Jesus, was without sin.
2. <u>Romans 6:23a.</u> What we earn by our sin is death, eternal separation from God.
3. <u>Romans 6:23b.</u> We earn death, but because of Christ, God gifts us with eternal life and presence with God.
4. <u>1 Peter 2:24.</u> Jesus bore our sin on the cross to relieve us of the penalty of sin.
5. <u>2 Corinthians 5:21.</u> God made Jesus, who was sinless, to bear our sin that we might become the righteousness of God. I call this the incredible exchange. God's righteousness assures our entry into God's Kingdom and eternal life, and we can't begin to earn or deserve this.
6. <u>Ephesians 2:8-9.</u> We are saved into eternal life through our faith in God's grace and the death, burial, and resurrection of Jesus. We can't do anything to earn this incredible gift.
7. <u>James 2:14-17.</u> Though we can't earn salvation, once we are saved, our eternal status as members of God's Kingdom will be revealed in the lives we live and the works we do. Faith must be followed by works.
8. <u>Mark 12:28-31.</u> Jesus sums up all the law (e.g., the Ten Commandments) and the prophets in these two commandments: love God and love people. Our mandate as followers of Christ is to love. I believe our love for others will be a demonstration of our love for God. <u>1 John 4:20</u> says that if we love God and hate our brother, we are liars. Everyone should be seen as our brother or neighbor. If we love God, we can't be choosy about who else we will love. Some might point out Luke 14:26, where Jesus says if we don't hate our family members, we can't be his disciples. We must understand that Jesus is talking comparatively here.

> Our love for Jesus should be so strong and active that it makes our love for family seem like hatred. Jesus and our lives lived for Him must be our priority.

These verses are a springboard. As you read and study Scripture, I'm sure you will find more.

What has Christ Done for You?

In John 3, Jesus talks to the Pharisee Nicodemus about being born again. Jesus says we can't see or be part of the Kingdom of God unless we are born again. Have you been born again? What evidence can you give of your new life in Christ?

I've discussed the beginning of my transformation in Christ: the awareness of a changed heart and the difficulty of the Lord ending my lying. Over the forty-some years since that time, I have seen God do so much in my life that I can't begin to recount it all. I would like to present two major — and more recent — activities of the Lord in my life.

A difficult relationship with my husband caused me to leave. After about nine months, the Lord made it clear that I was to return to my husband, and I did. For about 18 months, the Lord gave me the grace to walk with my husband through even more difficult times until he passed. I hadn't realized that many of the problems I had previously were because of the onset of dementia and other illnesses in his life.

The second major work of God in my life is teaching me about love. That may sound strange, but with what the Lord is showing me now, I realize that whatever feelings or attitudes I had previously were not love.

A life made new by Christ should result in many changes, both internally and externally. Sit down and list the changes that the Lord has brought into your life since you trusted in Christ.

What Do You Know About What Christ has Done for Others?

If you are in a fellowship of believers (church), you should see evidence—and hear stories—of what Christ has done for others. Perhaps you've seen new patience, caring, and awareness of the needs of others. Surely, you have heard stories of how the Lord has worked in the lives of some of your friends.

I was blessed to have people tell me about the changes they saw in me as I grew in faith and in my walk with the Lord. Being born again and the resulting transformation isn't a secret process. Just as others see a change in you, you should be seeing a change in others. Talk to people about what you see and what the Lord is doing in your life. This interaction can help you prepare to share your new life with others.

Questions for Consideration

1. What experiences with Christ have you had that can be helpful in discipling someone else?
2. How has what you have seen of Christ in others affected your life?

How Do You Share What You Know?

Scriptures: Matthew 10:16-33; Acts 2; 1 Peter 5:6-11

If we are learning about Christ and his redemptive work and growing in knowledge and faith but are not sharing our faith with others, we are not being good disciples. Jesus spent three years training a group of men who would become leaders in the creation and development of the Church. The Church, through the invasion of the Holy Spirit into these men, came into being because of their testimony. Our mission here on Earth is to be witnesses for Jesus so that the Church can continue until God's purpose and plan are fulfilled. There are several ways in which we can share the greatest message ever.

Christine Caine says that we have been sent into this world to represent Christ the King as ambassadors who represent the Kingdom of which we are citizens. As ambassadors of God's Kingdom,

1. We speak the message of God, who sends us (1 Corinthians 15:1-4);
2. We speak with the authority of God, who sends us (Matthew 28:18-20);
3. We are in constant communication with God, who sends us (1 Thessalonians 5:17);
4. We can bring heaven to earth as we pray and obey (Matthew 6:10);
5. We can bring the love of heaven into a world filled with hate;

6. We can bring kindness, goodness, faithfulness, gentleness, and self-control of the Spirit to a world so often starved of these things; and,
7. We can bring the comfort of God to hearts that are suffering.[5]

A Special Gift

If you are living in a vital, fulfilling relationship with God through the death, burial, and resurrection of Christ, you have a very precious and special gift. This gift is not to be hoarded or hidden under a bushel. It is to be shared with the world. Those who have this gift of God's grace are in the minority (Matthew 7:13-14). Many can give the impression of having this gift, but few are the ones who live in such a close relationship with Jesus that they are compelled to share the gift of Christ with others.

Lifestyle

I haven't heard the term "Lifestyle Evangelism" for a while, but this is my preferred style of sharing Christ with others.

Positive Aspects. A lifestyle of evangelism will speak of Christ in various ways. Regular, faithful attendance and participation in a community of faith is a strong beginning. A positive, encouraging attitude that avoids criticism and complaint is rare and will usually be noted by others. The love for God and all others will be clearly seen. Mercy and forgiveness will flow freely in the lives of faithful disciples.

Negative Aspects. Sadly, many people promote their relationship with Christ by the things they don't do. While we cannot live as citizens of this world, the Lord is not against our enjoyment of worldly activities, so long as the Lord is

---

5 Caine, Page 191.

always our priority. We are to be guided by the life of Christ. Jesus shared time with people who were considered unfit for society. Jesus joined in celebrations such as weddings and even provided refreshments, which would be deemed inappropriate in some Christian circles. Jesus did not avoid people who were considered as "other." If we truly follow Christ and desire to lead others to Christ, we won't be living a life based on things not to be done.

Charles Spurgeon says, "God has not commanded us to be diligent in making precepts, but in keeping them (Psalm 119:4). Some people bind yokes upon their own necks and make chains and rules for others, but the wise path is to be satisfied with the rules of Holy Scripture. Otherwise, we might become eminent in our own religion and fall short of acceptance by God." [6]

The Spoken Word

I can't deny that the most effective way of helping others find Christ is by the spoken word, backed up by a Godly lifestyle. If people can't see Jesus in our lives, it is unlikely they will listen to our words.

As a teacher, I share the message of Christ in a structured setting, and I prefer this. However, I have occasionally been led by the Lord to give testimony in an unstructured environment. While I will never become a street-corner preacher, I can be comfortable in such activity if I know the Holy Spirit is working and speaking through me.

It is important that when we witness to others and share the blessing of what Christ did for all, that we do so according to Scripture. We may think we know what Christ did in our lives, but we need to make sure that the sharing of that work

---

6 Spurgeon, Charles H. *The Golden Alphabet; An Exposition of Psalm 119*, Revised 2018, *Life Sentence Publishing*, Pg. 15.

is in line with Scripture. Many stories have come forth of what God did or will do that do not line up with Scripture. For example, God doesn't take babies because he needs another angel in heaven. God created angels, and they aren't babies. Nowhere in Scripture do we find that people become angels when they die. Make sure that any testimony you give about God is in line with Scripture.

Acts of Sharing

There is one aspect of lifestyle evangelism that I think deserves special attention: generosity. Jesus gave His all for humanity. We should do no less. Sharing of our financial resources, our time, and ourselves reflects God's love for others.

There are other ways to demonstrate generosity of spirit: putting others before us (e.g., grocery lines), a kind word of praise and/or thanksgiving, a gift to the needy, and even a smile can make a big difference in someone's life. They may even ask the source of your unusual behavior.

We can find a lot of reasons not to tell people about Jesus, but remember, we don't do this in our own power. Our ability to witness is based on the One who:

1. Never grows faint or weary (Isaiah 40:28).
2. Renews our strength as we wait on Him (Isaiah 40:31).
3. Is greater than he who is in the world (1 John 4:4).
4. Is strong when we are weak (2 Corinthians 12:10).
5. Is all strength (Psalm 147:5).
6. Makes us strong in the strength of His might (Ephesians 6:10), and
7. Has promised that He will never leave nor forsake us (Hebrews 13:5).[7]

---

7 Caine, pg. 176

8. With such help, we have no reason for not sharing the precious gifts we have been given.

Questions for Consideration

1. In what ways have you been an Ambassador for Christ?
2. Why do you share Christ with others?
3. Do you prefer speaking your message or living it out?
4. Are you generous with your resources of time, finances, and talent?

THE PROCESS CONTINUES

Scriptures: Romans 5:1-11; Revelation 2:7, 17, 26-29; 3:5, 12,
21 and Revelation 14:12.

Sadly, I have seen too many people who have made a profession of faith and attend church for a while, but then they fall away, often going back to a lifestyle that had no room for Christ. Are these people still headed for heaven? There is a lot of ambiguity in that question and a lot of different answers. Was their profession of faith sincere? Did they really receive Christ? Jesus' parable of the seed (Luke 8:4-15) gives us some insight. Some hear the Word and receive it with joy and believe for a while but then fall away. Others hear but are prevented from bearing fruit because of the cares of life. I believe that only those who continue with Christ and bear fruit are heaven-bound.

Many views of salvation are present in our world. John 3:16 (the Gospel in a nutshell) says it very plainly: whoever believes. What we truly believe will be demonstrated by our lives. We live what we believe. If our life here is not centered on Christ, I think it is highly unlikely we will spend eternity with Christ.

Salvation is Not a One Time Thing

Nowhere in Scripture do we find the idea of salvation as a one-time event. 1 Corinthians 15:2 speaks of the Gospel by which we are being saved, and that is conditional — we must hold fast to the Word. It is possible to believe in vain.

Salvation is a process that takes place from the time we first believe in Jesus until the time we see Jesus. We start in faith as we begin in life—by birth. First, our birth in the flesh. Then, when we receive Christ, we experience rebirth in the Spirit, when the Holy Spirit indwells us. Old things pass away and we are a new creation.

Then, just as in our natural life, we begin a learning process. Hebrews refers to the need for milk, not solid food, for the spiritually immature (Hebrews 5:11-14). Infants need milk. Solid food comes as we grow.

Just as we learn to walk by creeping, crawling, standing, and then taking baby steps, so we grow in Christ through learning the Scriptures, watching other believers, and determining to follow Jesus. This growth process is supplemented by prayer, worship, and continuing study of Scripture.

Don't Give Up

As we progress in our life in Christ—which I like to think of, and Scripture speaks of, as our "walk," e.g., 2 Corinthians 5:7—there will be obstacles that will come our way. Nothing will be too great for the Lord to help us overcome. However, early in our walk with the Lord, we may not be able to see the way and become discouraged.

The enemy used two people to try to discourage me in my early walk with the Lord. One was my mother. She thought that some choices I made in my new life were unnecessary. My mother didn't know the Lord, but she had a form of learned religion that satisfied her. The other discourager was a man at church who thought that the trials I experienced early in my faith walk were an indication that I didn't really know the Lord.

I am not sure how the Lord brought me through those times, but I know that my persistence in prayer and Scripture study was instrumental in the process. I didn't give up, and

The Process Continues

God certainly didn't give up on me. In fact, I think the trials I experienced early in my life with Jesus made me stronger in faith.

The enemy doesn't want us to be successful in our new life with Christ, especially if we had previously been his faithful servant. He will feed us lies, which we can extinguish with the shield of faith provided in the armor of God (Ephesians 6:13-18a). I take up the armor every day. Its purpose is to help us withstand the evil day. Don't give up! God has provided all the resources we need to remain faithful in our life with Christ.

Eternity Awaits

When we stand firm in our faith, we have an inestimable treasure awaiting us: life with Christ for all eternity. I've often wished that the Scriptures could give us more information about heaven, but what we know gives us a good start. According to Revelation 21:4, there will be no more tears, no death, no pain, and no mourning. Can you imagine?!

One thing we must remember is that the promise of eternity is for those who persevere in their faith. Jude 1:17-23 is a call to endurance. 1 Corinthians 15:2 speaks of holding fast to the Word of God, which is saving us. And 2 Timothy 2:12 reminds us that if we endure, we will reign with Jesus. If we continue to the end as faithful disciples of Jesus Christ and faithful adherents to the Scriptures, what awaits will do far more than make our faithfulness worthwhile.

Questions for Consideration

1. How would you describe the process of salvation?
2. Are you sometimes discouraged in your walk with the Lord? What do you do about discouragement?
3. Do you look forward to life with Jesus in eternity?

An Alphabetic Primer of Discipleship

A. Acceptance of Christ
B. Being born again
C. Conformation of life with Christ/Church
D. Devotional
E. Experiences of Faith
F. Faithfulness to Scripture/Fellowship
G. Godliness
H. Heaven Bound
I. Interests and Hobbies
J. Jesus First
K. Kinship with Christ
L. Love
M. Maturing in Christ
N. New Life
O. Offering of yourself
P. Patience
Q. Quiet Time
R. Remembrance, Regret, and Rejection
S. Strengths and Weaknesses/Scripture
T. Time and Tools
U. Understanding
V. Victory
W. Witnessing
Y. Yet to Come